HOUSTON
TEXAS

A PHOTOGRAPHIC PORTRAIT

PHOTOGRAPHY AND NARRATIVE BY

Eric W. Pohl

TWIN LIGHTS PUBLISHERS, ROCKPORT, MASSACHUSETTS

First published in the United States of
America by:

Twin Lights Publishers, Inc.
51 Broadway
Rockport, Massachusetts 01966
Telephone: (978) 546-7398
www.twinlightspub.com

ISBN: 978-1-934907-30-6

10 9 8 7 6 5 4 3 2 1

(opposite)
Fred Hartman Bridge

(frontispiece)
Houston Skyline

(jacket front)
Sesquicentennial Park Fountain

Book design by:
SYP Design & Production, Inc.
www.sypdesign.com

Printed in China

The origins of Houston echo from the wake of revolution and the birth of a fledging new republic called Texas. On the afternoon of April 21, 1836, General Sam Houston led the outnumbered Texian Army to victory over Mexican forces on the banks of the San Jacinto River. The newly formed Republic of Texas would soon give rise to prosperity and the emergence of new cities and towns.

That same year, two visionary real estate speculators from New York came to the area seeking to establish a new city. Brothers Augustus C. and John K. Allen purchased 6,642 acres on the banks of a muddy meandering creek called Buffalo Bayou. They officially named it Houston, and their vision would foster what would become the fourth largest city in America.

In 1845, Texas joined the U.S. becoming the 28th state in the Union. Rapid growth in the later 19th century brought technological advancements to Houston such as the railroad industry, the city's first power plant, paved roads, and electric street cars.

In 1901, oil was struck in East Texas and Houston would become the center of operations as enterprising entrepreneurs flooded the region. By 1929, forty oil companies had offices in Houston — securing the city's moniker as "The Energy Capital of the World."

The next few decades would witness the Port of Houston's expansive growth, the launch of NASA's manned space program, and the advancement of the Texas Medical Center — the world's largest medical complex.

Today, the "Bayou City" is a fast-paced international metropolis with world-class museums, a vibrant theater district, upscale shopping, and a highly acclaimed culinary scene.

In *Houston: A Photographic Portrait*, Eric Pohl captures the spirit and culture of the city through stunning photography. Houston's urban landscape comes to life through images highlighting the city's historic and modern architecture, beautiful parks, regional attractions, unique festivals, landmarks, and first-class venues for arts and entertainment.

Mist Tree (*opposite*)

Created by artist Doug Hollis, this stainless steel sculpture is the centerpiece of the Sarofim Picnic Lawn in Houston's Discovery Green Park. The piece features a mist cloud and a striking rain curtain falling from a circular pan.

Seven Wonders *(above)*

Rising above the Allen H. Carruth Promenade at Sesquicentennial Park, these 70-foot-tall pillars were created by architects Team HOU and artist Mel Chin. They highlight Houston's heritage through 1,050 children's drawings that have been laser-cut into steel plates.

Sesquicentennial Park Fountain *(opposite)*

This graceful park, in the heart of the downtown Theater District, celebrates Houston's sesquicentennial. Features of the park include a promenade overlooking Buffalo Bayou and a cascading multi-level fountain that follows the adjacent grand staircase as you enter the park.

Theater District (above)

Houston's renowned Theater District is home to an impressive assortment of entertainment venues. Within a few blocks are Jones Hall, Alley Theatre, Hobby Center for the Performing Arts, Bayou Place, and Wortham Theater Center.

Texas Flag (right)

An enduring symbol of Texas' fierce independent spirit, the Texas state flag dates back to 1839. Bearing the design of the last national flag of the Republic of Texas, the single star gave rise to the nickname, "The Lone Star State."

Sabine-to-Bagby Promenade (opposite)

A stroll across the Buffalo Bayou Pedestrian Bridge, connecting both sides of the Sabine-to-Bagby Promenade, offers great views of the skyline. The park's unique lighting changes from blue to white, in synch with the phases of the moon.

9

Light Rail *(above)*

Houston's light rail trains zip through downtown ferrying passengers across a water feature at Main Street Square. METRORail, Houston's ever-expanding light rail public transit system, opened in 2004.

Discovery Green Park *(left)*

Late afternoon sunlight filters through falling water created by *Mist Tree* at Discovery Green — Houston's premier downtown park. The stainless steel sculpture by San Francisco artist Doug Hollis has become an attraction for the park as children and adults alike enjoy the cooling water feature.

Light Rail Fountain *(opposite)*

Houston's downtown light rail system comes to life with an impressive water feature installed on Main Street Square. METRORail trains travel through a 250-foot-long reflection pool with a symphony of 40-foot-tall arching water jets and vibrant colored lights.

Brown Foundation Promenade

Featuring student photography, the Brown
Foundation Promenade at Discovery
Green Park is adorned with internally-lit
globes suspended from 100-year-old
live oak trees. *Through the Eyes of a Child*
was created in partnership with Artist
David Graeve and Buffalo Bayou Art Park.

DISCOVERY GREEN

Discovery Green

From interactive waterscapes and iconic public art to restaurants and an urban market, Discovery Green is Houston's premier urban park. Opened in 2008, this remarkable 12-acre green space adds character to the heart of downtown Houston.

Heritage Lanterns

Commissioned in 2005, *Heritage Lanterns* adorn the northeast corner of Root Memorial Park in downtown Houston. Created by artists Carter Ernst and Paul Kittelson, these striking Victorian-style stainless steel spires are internally lit and resemble illuminated rooftops.

Bayou Place

Located in the heart of Houston's vibrant downtown Theater District, Bayou Place is a thriving venue for live music, dining, bars, and entertainment. With a variety of offerings, the $22-million-dollar Bayou Place complex is a one-stop shop for Houston's weekend nightlife.

Williams Tower *(opposite)*

Decked out in holiday flare, the iconic 64-story Williams Tower soars over Houston's Galleria Mall and Uptown District. Beginning on Thanksgiving Day each year, decorations and dozens of twinkling holiday trees flank Post Oak Boulevard.

Williams Waterwall *(top)*

Reminiscent of an ancient Roman theatre, water tumbles down through channels on a semi-circular wall and over descending steps at 11,000 gallons per minute. The Williams Waterwall stands at 64-feet-tall, representative of the adjacent 64-story Williams Tower.

GRB Convention Center *(bottom)*

One of the largest meeting facilities in the U.S., the George R. Brown Convention Center is a premier venue for conferences, expositions, and more. Its central location is convenient to Minute Maid Park, Toyota Center, Discovery Green, as well as upscale hotels.

Buffalo Bayou *(top)*

Commercial shipping on Buffalo Bayou was crucial to Houston's early economic growth in the 1800's. Today, the bayou is a quiet waterway flanked by hike and bike trails as it meanders through downtown, Memorial Park, and historic neighborhoods such as River Oaks.

Buffalo Bayou Park *(bottom)*

With great views of downtown, Buffalo Bayou Park greenbelt winds along both sides of the bayou. It features a disc golf course, canoe launch sites, and public art and connects multiple green spaces such as Eleanor Tinsley Park — home to Houston's Fourth of July celebration.

Market Square Clock *(opposite)*

This 1904 clock originally adorned one of Houston's early City Hall buildings. In 1996, the clock was installed in its current home, the Louis and Annie Friedman Clock Tower across from Market Square Park.

Sabine Street Bridge *(above)*

One of the most photographed bridges in Houston, the Sabine Street Bridge gracefully spans 240 feet over Buffalo Bayou. Completed in 1924, it's adorned with ornate urn style balustrades.

Memorial Park *(right)*

Popular among joggers, thousands of Houstonians hit the trails of Memorial Park daily. It's one of the nation's largest parks, situated on the original site of Camp Logan — a World War I Army training camp. Park amenities include tennis courts, a 600-acre golf course, and an arboretum.

Hermann Park *(opposite)*

One of Houston's most celebrated public spaces, 445-acre Hermann Park is home to a golf course, a reflection pond, the Miller Outdoor Theatre, Japanese Gardens, the Houston Zoo, the Houston Museum of Natural Science, the Houston Garden Center, a railroad, and more.

George Hermann

A 1981 bronze statue by Lonnie Edwards commemorates George H. Hermann — who in 1914 gifted 285 acres to the city of Houston for recreational use as Pines Park. That same year, Hermann passed away and the city expanded the plan and renamed the space Hermann Park.

McGovern Lake

With grand views of the Texas Medical
Center, McGovern Lake is a central feature
of Hermann Park. Explore the lake in one
of the park's pedal boats or stroll around
this 8-acre lake to enjoy the exceptional
migratory bird watching.

Houston Arboretum and Nature Center

A couple strolls down a wooded nature trail under a springtime canopy in the Houston Arboretum and Nature Center. This 155-acre reserve features a nature center, classes for children and adults, and miles of trails that take you through various native ecological habitats.

Wildlife in Hermann Park *(top and bottom)*

A variety of waterfowl such as black-bellied whistling-ducks and mammals like nutria call Hermann Park home year-round. Seasonal migratory birds can be seen on two of the three islands on McGovern Lake.

Sam Houston Park *(above and opposite)*

Modern glass and steel of Houston's skyline tower over the city's oldest public park. Originally called City Park when it opened in 1899, it was later renamed Sam Houston Park. Features include lush green space, a gazebo, water features, monuments, and several historic 19th-century buildings.

Sundial *(right)*

This sculpture in Sam Houston Park, *Houston Armillary Sphere* has a 72-inch diameter with a large vertical ring representing the meridian of Houston. A central rod points toward the North Star. An outer band, representing the celestial equator, is etched with zodiac symbols.

City Hall and Reflection Pool *(above)*

Literally in the shadow of towering skyscrapers, Houston's 1939 modernistic deco-style City Hall overlooks Hermann Square and a reflection pool in down-town. Still the center of city business, it is home to the Mayor's Office, City Council Chamber, and the Houston Visitors Center.

Sam Houston Monument *(opposite)*

Unveiled in 1925, this 40-foot bronze equestrian figure of Sam Houston is one of Hermann Park's most prominent features. Donated by the Women's City Club of Houston and sculpted by Enrico Filiberto Cerracchio, the statue sits atop a gray granite masonry arch by Frank Teich.

Tranquility Park *(top)*

Dedicated on the tenth anniversary of the 1979 Apollo 11 mission, Tranquility Park commemorates the moon landing. Located across from City Hall, the park's multi-level cascading oasis — Wortham Fountain — and earthworks represent the Apollo rockets and the moon's surface.

Wortham Park *(bottom and opposite)*

The Gus S. and Lyndall F. Wortham Park is 1.2 acres of serenity in the heart of the Texas Medical Center. Green space, trees, and rows of tapering water columns sit adjacent to a colonnade of vine-covered pergolas flanking a 650-foot-long pool with dancing water spouts.

Doric Columns

A limestone colonnade surrounds a circular pool and fountain, forming this 1968 monument in Hermann Park. The perimeter of the Mecom-Rockwell Fountain and Colonnade is constructed of Doric columns salvaged from Houston's original Miller Outdoor Theatre.

Niels Esperson Building (*opposite*)

The tallest building in Texas upon its opening in 1927, this ornate structure was built by Mellie Esperson in honor of her late husband, oil and land tycoon, Niels Esperson. Designed by architect John Eberson, its Italian Renaissance architecture still dazzles Houstonians today.

Houston Center (*top*)

Nestled in downtown's dynamic East End, Houston Center is a multi-building upscale retail, office, and shopping complex. It includes the 52-floor Fulbright Tower and The Shops at Houston Center with first-class shopping and the largest food court in Texas.

Downtown Tunnels (*bottom*)

Beneath Houston's downtown streets is a matrix of more than six miles of pedestrian tunnels that connect 95 city blocks. From a multitude of entry points, shops, restaurants, retail spaces, and more are accessible in these climate-controlled subterranean walkways.

Old Courthouse *(above)*

Harris County Courthouse has endured many transitions, but today it stands as a reminder of the past. Modernization projects in 1954 removed much of the ornate interior — including marble walls and a dome skylight. In 2011, it was restored to its original 1910 grandeur.

Sweeney Clock *(right)*

This historic downtown landmark is a relic of the early 1900's in Houston. Made of thick cast-iron, this Victorian-style clock was originally located on Main Street in front of the Sweeney Jewelry store. In the mid-1970's, it was moved to its current location at Capitol and Bagby streets.

New Courthouse *(opposite)*

The 17-story, state-of-the-art Harris County Civil Courthouse was opened in 2006. The building features a pre-cast concrete exterior, a copper domed rotunda, and a basement connecting by tunnel to the adjacent Harris County Jury Plaza building.

Sky Lobby (top)

For a bird's-eye view of Houston, look no further than the Sky Lobby in the JPMorgan Chase Tower. Built in 1982, the 60th floor observation deck provides the highest public view in the city with visibility of more than 20 miles on a clear day.

Personage and Birds (bottom)

The focal point of the plaza at JPMorgan Chase Tower is a freestanding 55-foot-tall steel and cast bronze sculpture by Spanish artist Joan Miró. Dedicated in 1982, *Personage and Birds* is scaled from a smaller bronze version that's on display in the tower's Sky Lobby, 60 floors above.

JPMorgan Chase Tower (opposite)

Originally known as Texas Commerce Tower, the 75-story pentagonal building was completed in 1981 and stands as the tallest building in Texas. The 85-foot-wide glass main entry was designed to harmonize with the portico of Jones Hall, across the street.

Houston Medical Center *(left)*

Home to many prestigious medical facilities, the Texas Medical Center has become the world's largest medical complex. Founded in 1945, the TMC began improvements on 134 undeveloped acres that the M.D. Anderson Foundation purchased from the city the previous year.

The Commons *(right)*

Opened in 2002, the John P. McGovern Texas Medical Center Common's two 55-foot-tall waterfalls cleverly disguise a parking garage and amenities on 6 levels. Designed by Jackson & Ryan Architects, it includes a food court, bank, florist, and an upscale restaurant on the top level.

The Health Museum

Walk through a larger-than-life human body, see dissections of real organs, or get interactive with science labs at the John P. McGovern Museum of Health & Medical Science. Originally part of the Houston Museum of Natural Science, this innovative learning center opened in 1996.

Pennzoil Place *(opposite)*

One of the pioneering structures of the postmodernism era, Pennzoil Place is comprised of two 36-story trapezoidal towers. A 155-foot-tall glass-enclosed courtyard joins the towers. Designed by famed architects Philip Johnson and John Burgee, it was completed in 1975.

MD Anderson Cancer Center *(top)*

In 1941, the MD Anderson Foundation and the state of Texas funded the establishment of Texas' first cancer hospital. Today, the University of Texas MD Anderson Cancer Center is the world's largest freestanding cancer center and a leader in comprehensive care and research.

Jones Hall for the Performing Arts *(bottom)*

Home to the Houston Symphony and Society for the Performing Arts since 1966, Jones Hall's award-winning design features a grand lobby with high ceilings and three tiered terraces The multi-story portico and white Italian marble exterior are instantly recognizable in downtown Houston.

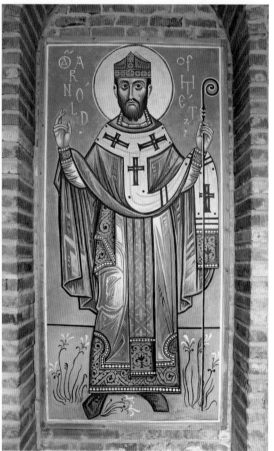

Saint Arnold's Brewery *(above and left)*

Since 1994, Saint Arnold's Brewery has been producing a variety of award-winning beers, including seasonal specialties at their microbrewery near downtown Houston. The brewery, named after the Patron Saint of Brewers, is open to the public for tours and beer tastings in their grand beer hall.

Galleria Mall *(opposite)*

Texas' largest shopping center, the Galleria Mall is the jewel of Houston's Uptown District. This popular tourist destination is crowned by a barrel vault atrium skylight and offers hundreds of retail and dining choices, plus a 20,000-square-foot indoor ice-skating rink.

Gus S. Wortham Memorial Fountain

Architect William T. Cannady designed this impressive lacquer-coated bronze fountain that has prominently graced the south bank of Buffalo Bayou since 1978. Surrounded by a tiered circular pool, a bouquet of sprinkler tubes radiate from a central shaft spraying a sphere of water and mist.

Wortham Theater Center *(top and bottom)*

Home to the Houston Ballet and Houston Grand Opera, the Wortham Theater Center debuted in 1987. It was designed by architect Eugene Aubry and funded by private donations. Located in the Theater District, the center's plaza offers views of Sesquicentennial Park and Buffalo Bayou.

Houston Visitors Center *(above)*

Located on the first floor of Houston's historic City Hall building, the Houston Visitors Center is part museum, part gift shop, and part information desk. Features include historical and cultural exhibits, a small theater, brochures, and a helpful staff with expert advice on local attractions.

Chinatown *(left and opposite)*

Houston's unique diversity includes a vibrant Asian population — America's second-largest Indochinese community. Houston's Chinatown is a thriving Asian cultural mecca in southwest Houston, encompassing six square miles of Asian-oriented businesses like Hong Kong City Mall — the largest indoor Asian mall in the southwestern U.S.

Houston Heights *(above)*

Distinguished by its historic charm, eclectic style and sense of community, the Houston Heights District is one of the city's most desirable neighborhoods. Old meets new as early 20th-century craftsman-style bungalows and colorful Queen Anne Victorians mingle with modern townhomes.

Old Town Spring *(left)*

Once a booming railroad town, Spring was platted in 1873, just north of Houston. Today, the Old Town Spring district attracts Houstonians with its quaint tree-lined streets, Victorian-style shops, restaurants, art galleries, and events like the Texas Crawfish and Music Festival.

Victorians *(above and right)*

Just south of the Houston area, the island city of Galveston is home to a medley of well-preserved 19th-century Victorian buildings including the 1889 24,000-square-foot George Sealy Mansion (above) and the 1896 Hutchings Sealy Building (right).

Julia Ideson Library *(above)*

This wonderful Spanish Renaissance-style building was erected in 1926 under the direction of Houston's first head librarian and the building's namesake. From 1903–1945, Julia Ideson directed the expansion of Houston's Carnegie Library into a multi-branch public library system.

Clayton Library *(opposite, top)*

Originally housed in the Julia Ideson Building, the Houston Public Library's genealogical research collection was moved and became the Clayton Library Center for Genealogical Research in 1968. The adjacent Main Building was later opened in 1988.

Czech Center Museum *(opposite, bottom)*

Incorporated in 1996, the Czech Center Museum features permanent exhibits of paintings, Moravian hand-painted pottery, Czech porcelain and ceramics, antique furniture from European castles, Bohemian crystal, and more. The center also offers genealogical research and event spaces.

1940 Air Terminal Museum

Located at William P. Hobby Airport, this historic 1940 art deco building was the original Houston Municipal Airport control tower. It now houses a collection of civil aviation heritage displays, memorabilia, and several planes including a Hawker business jet and an airworthy Lockheed Lodestar.

Kemah Boardwalk Marina

In a business metropolis like Houston, Houstonians work hard and know how to play hard, too. Just south of Houston, the Clear Lake and Kemah area is home to the third largest number of recreational boats in the U.S.

Petroleum Refineries *(top and opposite)*

Houston's growth in shipping commodities on Buffalo Bayou necessitated a new deep-water port, which opened in 1914. Today, the Port of Houston is one of the world's largest ports and home to the world's second largest petrochemical complex.

Galveston Island *(bottom)*

Just south of Houston, the beaches of Galveston Island have long been a summer playground for Houstonians. From historic treasures like the Strand District to shopping, entertainment, beachfront dining, and first-class lodging, Galveston offers something for everyone.

Houston Ship Channel (*above*)

The 52-mile-long Houston Ship Channel is a large vessel water passage connecting the Port of Houston to Galveston Bay. It is home to many industrial facilities, petro-chemical refineries, and cargo terminals. The channel is 530 feet wide—allowing passage of container vessels, barges, tankers, and tugs.

Disney Magic (*left*)

A crowd gathers at Pier 21 on Galveston Island to wish bon voyage to friends and family aboard the 2700-passenger luxury cruise liner, *Disney Magic*. Galveston's cruise terminal is a major hub for cruise lines with destinations including Mexico, Central America, Jamaica, the Bahamas, and beyond.

Battleship Texas

Commissioned in 1914, the USS *Texas* played key roles in both World Wars. The *Texas* was the first U.S. battleship to mount anti-aircraft guns and the first to launch an aircraft from a catapult. The famed ship is now a floating museum moored just south of Houston.

San Jacinto Monument *(above and opposite)*

A tribute to the defining battle of the Texas Revolution, this 570-foot-tall monument overlooks the 1836 battleground and 1200-acre park. Behind its limestone walls and art deco friezes are an impressive history museum and an observation deck just beneath the 220-ton lone star.

Glenwood Cemetery

The lush grounds and curving roads of the cemetery are the resting place of Houston's elite. The Allen brothers, the city's founders, are buried here—along with prominent congressmen, governors, mayors, famed architects, and founders of some of the world's largest companies.

A 19th-Century Park

Long before Houston's first public park was developed, Glenwood Cemetery doubled as a recreational destination. Visitors took street cars to the cemetery to enjoy the garden-like landscaping. Today, visitors peruse the historical markers, Victorian headstones, and mausoleums.

Bayou Bend Collection and Gardens

(above and opposite)

Bayou Bend is the former family home of philanthropist Ima Hogg. Opened to the public in 1966, the John F. Staub designed home now houses the Museum of Fine Arts Houston's early American decorative arts and painting collection.

Bayou Bend Collection and Gardens

Philanthropist Ima Hogg — whose family co-developed River Oaks and donated the land for Memorial Park — had a love for gardening and natural beauty. Miss Hogg installed a variety of beautiful formal gardens, sculptures, and fountains on 14 acres that still amaze visitors today.

Museum of Fine Arts *(top and bottom)*

The south side of the Caroline Wiess Law Building showcases the original 1924 neo-classical museum designed by architect William Ward Watkin. The contrastingly modern north end (bottom) welcomes visitors to the museum's main campus and houses some of its premier collections.

Cullen Sculpture Garden *(top)*

The Lillie and Hugh Roy Cullen Sculpture Garden offers a harmonious fusion of art and nature in the heart of Houston's Museum District. Take a stroll through sculpted works by renowned 20th- and 21st-century artists in the company of architectural walls and tranquil landscaping.

Rienzi Mansion *(bottom)*

Designed in 1952 by prominent architect John F. Staub, Rienzi Mansion is the former home of philanthropists Carroll Sterling Masterson and Harris Masterson III. The home now houses the Museum of Fine Arts, Houston's European decorative arts and paintings collection.

Mecom Fountain (*above*)

Installed in 1964, the *Mecom Fountain* majestically greets visitors at the entrance to Hermann Park. The fountain was gifted to the city by Mary and John W. Mecom, Sr. Designed by Eugene Werlin, its dancing water gushes atop a base of white marble and cycles 8,000 gallons per minute.

Hobby Center (*opposite*)

Opened in 2002, the Hobby Center for the Performing Arts elevates Houston's Theater District with its brilliant design by architect Robert A. M. Stern. It features 60-foot-high glass walls, a second floor terrace, two theaters, a restaurant, and modern art including *In Minds*, by Tony Cragg.

Jung Center

Educational programs in psychology, spirituality, and the arts and humanities are cornerstones of the C. G. Jung Educational Center of Houston. Founded in 1958, this unique institute offers classes, workshops, a bookstore, museum, gallery, and exhibits emphasizing the human spirit.

HOLOCAUST MUSEUM HOUSTON

Educational Centre and Memorial

A living testimonial to those who died. A place to honor those who survived, and a source of education for present and future generations

Holocaust Museum

Honoring the millions of Holocaust victims, the Holocaust Museum Houston is committed to educating people about the atrocities of genocide. Among the museum's exhibits is an authentic 1942 World War II railcar — the type used for Nazi concentration camp transportation.

Colorful Crosswalk *(top)*

Houston's METRORail speeds past a colorful pedestrian crosswalk in the Museum District. Visitors leaving the Museum of Fine Arts affectionately place their museum lapel stickers on a utility pole near the museum.

Museum District *(bottom)*

Houston's world-class Museum District attracts visitors from all over with its diverse collection of culture, art, history, spirituality, and science centers. The district is also home to Rice University, the Miller Outdoor Theatre, the Houston Zoo, and Hermann Park (pictured).

Buffalo Soldiers *(top and bottom)*

Housed in the 1925 Houston Light Guard Armory, the Buffalo Soldiers National Museum celebrates the legacy of African American military service. Founded in 2000 by Vietnam veteran and military historian, Captain Paul J. Matthews it features exhibits, memorabilia and artifacts.

Children's Museum of Houston

Innovative and engaging, the Children's Museum of Houston is packed with interactive learning exhibits that spark kids' curiosities. Founded in 1980, this whimsical learning center was designed by noted architect, Robert Venturi.

Children's Zoo

From a petting zoo and a bat cave to a butterfly pavilion and playground, the John P. McGovern Children's Zoo gives children a chance to learn about animals up close in an interactive environment.

Downtown Aquarium *(above and opposite)*

Landry's Downtown Aquarium spans
six acres in Houston's Theater District. In
addition to a restaurant and upscale bar,
attractions include an amusement park
and an array of aquariums and wildlife
exhibits featuring sharks, a 20-foot-long
python, and a pair of white tigers.

Butterfly Center *(above and opposite)*

Butterflies abound as you roam the incredible Rain Forest Conservatory's three-story glass structure at the Houston Museum of Natural Science Cockrell Butterfly Center. The adjacent Brown Hall of Entomology exhibits mounted butterflies and offers interactive games and more.

Morian Hall of Paleontology
(above and right)

Wander through dozens of dinosaur and large mammal skeletons posed in lifelike action scenarios. The Morian Hall of Paleontology at the Museum of Natural Science features hundreds of fossils, an extraordinary collection of petrified wood (bottom), and even fossilized dinosaur skin.

Museum of Natural Science *(opposite)*

Founded in 1909, the Houston Museum of Natural Science is one of the nation's most visited museums. Among its halls are the Wortham Theatre, Cockrell Butterfly Center, and the state-of-the-art Burke Baker Planetarium (opposite). Exhibits include gems and minerals, ancient culture, chemistry, ecology, and more.

Houston Fire Museum *(above and left)*

Fire Station No. 7 was the first station built after Houston's Fire Department became city operated in 1898. Now housing the Houston Fire Museum, visitors can see a 1937 pumper truck and horse-drawn steamer or learn how fireman lived and worked between 1899 to 1969.

National Museum of Funeral History

One of Houston's most unique attractions, the museum houses a collection of funeral service artifacts and masterfully designed funerary customs exhibits. Featured are historic hearses, authentic American presidential funeral artifacts, and the original Popemobile used by John Paul II.

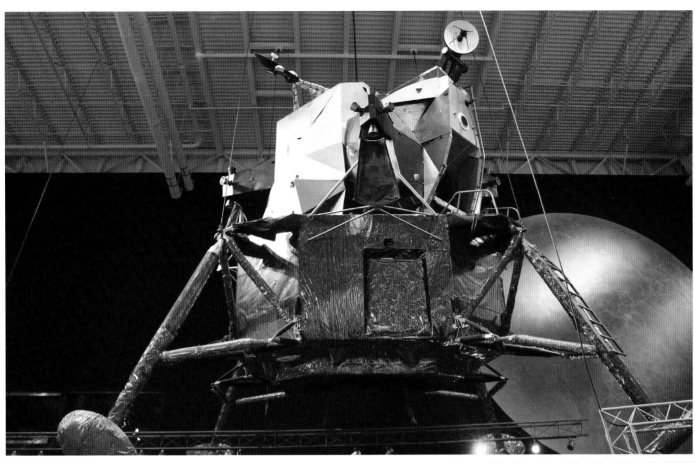

Johnson Space Center *(above and right)*

The Lyndon B. Johnson Space Center opened in 1963 and from the Gemini and Apollo missions to the Space Shuttle and International Space Station, JSC continues as the forefront of manned space exploration. Visitors are treated to exhibits, theaters, and interactive learning for kids.

Building 9 *(opposite)*

For a deeper exploration, Space Center Houston visitors can embark on a tram tour of the JSC campus, including historic Mission Control, Rocket Park, the International Space Station trainer, the Neutral Buoyancy Lab, and Building 9 — NASA's Vehicle Mock-Up Facility.

Rocket Park *(above and left)*

Space Center Houston's Rocket Park wows visitors as they see real historic NASA rockets up close. Highlights include the *Little Joe II* rocket (above left), *Mercury Redstone 7* rocket (above right) and the colossal *Saturn V* rocket (left) — 36 stories tall — used in the Apollo missions.

Little Joe II Rocket *(opposite)*

Unmanned test launches were conducted in White Sands Missile Range from 1963-1966. The *Little Joe II* rocket and the BP22 unmanned capsule were part of tests confirming the rocket and capsule design viability and paving the way for NASA's manned space program.

Tolerance (*opposite*)

Dedicated in 2011, *Tolerance* consists of seven aluminum-framed human figures comprised of letters in several languages and representing the seven continents. Created by Spanish artist, Jaume Plensa, they adorn a prominent recreation area at Harmony Walk on Buffalo Bayou.

Beer Can House (*above*)

This folk-art landmark is a house that's been covered and decorated with beer cans, bottles, marbles, and trinkets. It was created by retired upholsterer John Milkovisch over a 20-year period and is now operated by the Orange Show Center for Visionary Art.

Menil Collection

From antiquities and medieval art to modern and contemporary art, the Menil Collection, opened in 1987, houses a diverse array of world art. The unique museum building, with curved leaf skylights and enclosed gardens, was designed by renowned Italian architect Renzo Piano.

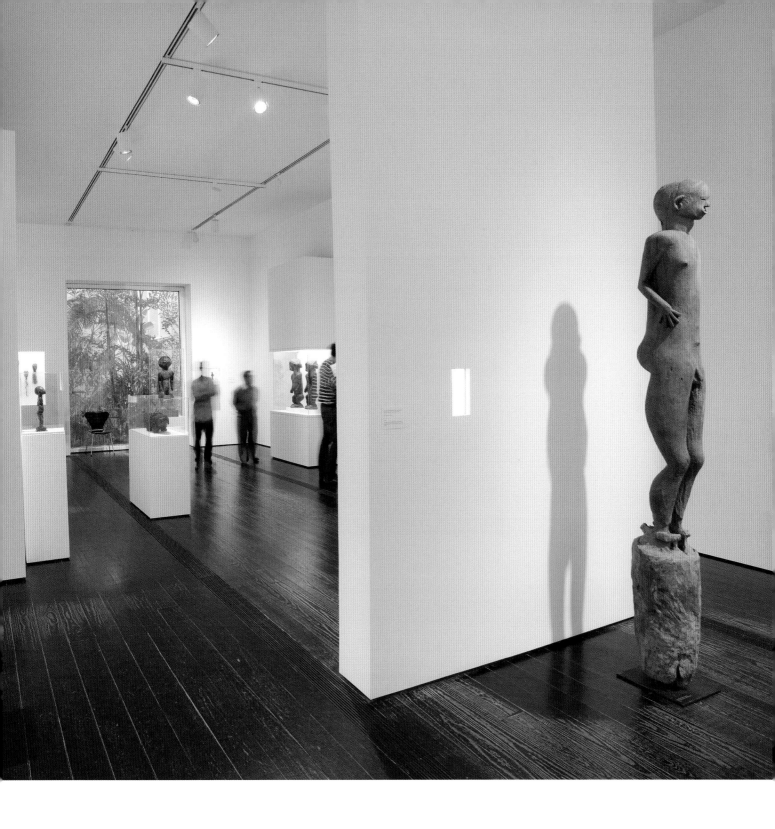

Giant President Heads (*above*)

Best known for large sculptural works, including a 67-foot-tall statue of Sam Houston, David Adickes' workshop has become an offbeat tourist destination. Forty-three giant presidential busts, originally intended for a defunct park project, now adorn the studio parking lot.

Virtuoso and Lyric Center (*opposite*)

Commissioned in 1983, *The Virtuoso* is a 36-foot-tall cellist sculpture created by artist David Adickes. The sculpture graces the plaza of the Lyric Center, an office building in downtown Houston.

Rice University *(above and opposite)*

One of the nation's top academic institutions, Rice University opened in 1912 and is named for businessman William Marsh Rice. The iconic Byzantine-style Lovett Hall, designed by architect Ralph Adams Cram, is named for the university's visionary first president, Edgar Odell Lovett.

University of Houston

The University of Houston, the city's leading public research and teaching institution, was founded in 1927. *Tower of the Cheyenne*, a 1972 sculpture by Peter Forakis, is featured in front of the M.D. Anderson Library.

University of Houston-Downtown *(above)*

Located on Buffalo Bayou, the historic UH One Main Building began its life as the Merchants and Manufacturers Building in 1930 — a unique art deco-style combination office and warehouse. It later became South Texas Junior College before being acquired by the University of Houston System in 1974.

Houston Cougars *(right)*

The cougar was adopted as the official mascot of the University of Houston in 1947. Students symbolically rub the paws of the two statues in front of the E. Cullen Building for good luck before a big game or important test.

Heritage Society *(above and opposite)*

Set among the tranquil backdrop of Sam Houston Park, the Heritage Society exhibits and preserves historic Houston structures. Their collection features homes and buildings dating from 1823 to 1905, including the Nichols-Rice-Cherry House (pictured), once owned by William Marsh Rice.

Palmer Memorial Episcopal Church
(above)

Designed by famed architect William Ward Watkin, the church was originally a complex that included female dormitories and a collegiate chapel. Dedicated in 1927, it bears the name of the benefactor's brother, Edward Albert Palmer.

St. John Church *(opposite)*

The glass and steel of Houston's skyline stands juxtaposed over historic St. John Church. Built by German farmers in 1891, the evangelical Lutheran church was later donated to the Houston Heritage Society and moved to Sam Houston Park in 1968.

First United Methodist Church (left)

Tracing its congregation's roots back to 1837, the church opened services in downtown under the name Methodist Episcopal Church South. The church moved to its current sanctuary in 1910 and the name changed to First United Methodist Church in 1968.

St. Paul Methodist Church (right)

This iconic 1930 English Gothic church is home to St. Paul Methodist Church, a congregation dating back to 1905. The building features a limestone exterior with slate roof and was designed by architect Alfred C. Finn, designer of the San Jacinto Monument.

Antioch Missionary Baptist Church (opposite)

Nestled among towering skyscrapers in downtown Houston, Antioch Missionary Baptist Church was built in 1875. This historic congregation was organized by a group of freed slaves in 1866 and became the center of African-American life in late 19th-century Houston.

Mormon Temple

Opened in 2000, the Houston Texas Temple was the second Church of Jesus Christ of Latter-day Saints temple to be built in Texas. The striking Luna pearl granite structure graces 11 beautifully landscaped acres in northwest Houston.

Rothko Chapel

Since 1971, the Rothko Chapel, founded
by John and Dominique de Menil, has
been a sanctuary for people of all beliefs.
Its meditative spaces harmonize with ab-
stract murals by artist Mark Rothko. Barnett
Newman's steel sculpture, *Broken Obelisk*,
is dedicated to Dr. Martin Luther King, Jr.

Christ Church Cathedral *(above and left)*

The 1839 formation of Christ Church Cathedral established Houston's first religious congregation. The current 1893 Gothic Revival sanctuary showcases ornate woodwork and an authentic Tiffany drapery glass window.

Greek Festivals

Celebrating Greek culture with authentic cuisine, dancing and activities, the Original Greek Festival is held annually at Houston's Annunciation Greek Orthodox Cathedral. This 1952 Byzantine-style cathedral is home to one of the nation's largest orthodox churches, which was formed 1917.

Bayou City Art Festival

The biannual Bayou City Art Festival began as a community arts and crafts event in 1971, growing in popularity over the years. The current name was adopted in 1997 and today it attracts artists from all over North America, including Kimber Fiebiger and her whimsical sculptures.

Texas Renaissance Festival *(top and bottom)*

Jousting knights, street musicians, and hundreds of other costumed performers enchant visitors at the Texas Renaissance Festival. Touted as the country's largest renaissance festival, each fall the 55-acre medieval European village is host to arts, crafts, and food vendors.

The Woodlands (opposite)

Founded in 1974 by developer George P. Mitchell, this master-planned suburban community has grown into an attractive township with its appealing developments and downtown waterway. Located just north of Houston, it is home to several corporate campuses and headquarters.

Freedom Over Texas (top)

Houston's downtown skyline comes to life as a brilliant display of patriotic pyrotechnics soar over the city. The annual fireworks are perfectly timed to patriotic music selections. Attracting more than 100,000 people, the event includes free educational and entertainment programs.

Ballunar Liftoff (bottom)

Blazing hot air balloons illuminate the night at the annual Ballunar Liftoff Festival. Celebrating manned flight, the family festival draws crowds of Houstonians to the Johnson Space Center for balloon flights, sky diver exhibitions, hang gliders, model rockets, and a NASA open house.

Galveston Pleasure Pier *(above and opposite)*

With classic amusement rides, midway games and unforgettable ocean views, the Galveston Pleasure Pier teems with nostalgic family fun. Opened in 2012 by Landry's Inc., the pier harkens back to the original Galveston Pleasure Pier of the 1940's, which shut down after hurricane damage in 1961.

We Love Houston (above)

Houston artist David Adickes' *We (Heart) Houston* sculpture is a large public art display facing Interstate 10 near downtown. Standing at 30 feet, this three-dimensional love letter to Houston was dedicated in 2013.

The Orange Show (left and opposite)

A folk-art monument of architecture and found objects, The Orange Show is a jumble of ornately adorned walkways, verandas, and one-of-a-kind exhibits. From 1956 until his death in 1980, Jeff McKissack built and painted this solitary tribute to his favorite fruit.

Kemah Boardwalk

A seaside getaway on Galveston Bay, the Landry's Inc. Kemah Boardwalk offers themed waterfront restaurants and entertainment such as amusement rides, midway games, performances, and live animal exhibits. The 60-acre complex also has retail stores, a marina, and a boutique hotel.

Reflection Pool

Lined with benches and shaded by live
oak trees, the 90,000-gallon Reflecting
Pool at Houston Zoo is stocked with
more than 200 Koi. These colorful fish
grow to be up to 30 inches long and can
weigh up to 15 pounds.

Houston Zoo *(above and right)*

Visitors can take a journey around the world with more than 6000 exotic animals from every corner of the globe at the Houston Zoo. Founded in 1922, the 55-acre zoo is conveniently located within Hermann Park.

Houston Astros Tribute *(bottom and opposite)*

Adjacent to Minute Maid Park, Halliburton Plaza is a 27,000-square-foot outdoor space featuring public art and commemorative displays celebrating the Houston Astros. The action-posed Jeff Bagwell statue (opposite) was created by Robert Hogan.

Minute Maid Park *(top)*

A fully retractable roof and retro-styled architecture are distinguishing features of the 40,000-seat Minute Maid Park. Home of the Houston Astros, it opened in 2000 on the site of historic Union Station and features a moving 50,000-pound locomotive used for home run celebrations.

Reliant Stadium *(opposite)*

Home to the NFL's Houston Texans, Reliant Stadium features a retractable roof, a natural grass field, and a seating capacity of 71,500. The stadium's flexible design allows configuration for a multitude of events including the Houston Livestock Show and Rodeo.

Toyota Center *(top and bottom)*

Houston's downtown Toyota Center is home to the Houston Rockets basketball team and host to large concerts as a premiere live entertainment venue. The center opened in 2003, spans six city blocks, and seats up to 19,000.

Sam Houston Race Park *(above and left)*

Visitors revel in the fast action thrill of thoroughbred and quarter horse racing at Sam Houston Race Park in northwest Houston. The park opened in 1994 and offers a glass walled grandstand, luxury suites with trackside views, and onsite dining options.

Rodeo Houston *(above)*

With a rich heritage founded in 1931, the Houston Livestock Show and Rodeo has grown to become the world's largest rodeo. The show features action-packed bull riding, team roping and chuck wagon races (pictured), as well as barbecue cook offs, a huge carnival, shopping, and concerts.

Trail Riders *(right)*

Trail riders head into downtown Houston to kick off the Houston Livestock Show and Rodeo. A tradition dating to 1952, hundreds of men, women, and children ride horseback or wagon from varying distances around Texas, the longest being from Reynosa, Mexico.

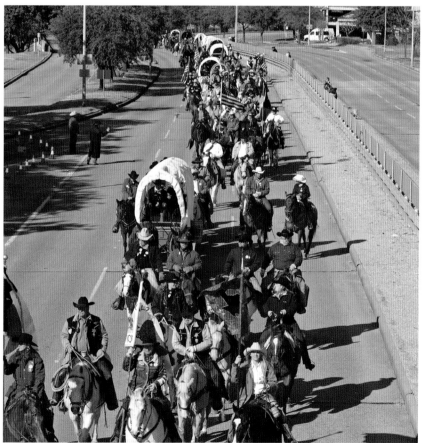

Eric W. Pohl

Eric W. Pohl is an award-winning photographer and freelance writer specializing in Texas travel and outdoors. From the natural landscape to the urban landscape, he harnesses the perfect light and a unique perspective to tell his visual story. It's through his vibrant images and writings that he shares his passion for the spirited history and culture of the "Lone Star State."

Eric's photos and articles have appeared in numerous books, websites and magazines including *Camping Life, Here Is Houston, Houston Business Journal, Nature Friend, Texas Highways, Texas Live* and *Wildflower.*

Native to Houston, Eric now lives in Austin with his wife and three dogs. In addition to his commercial, editorial, and fine art photography, he also works as a graphic designer and web professional.

For more information about Eric, including photographic prints of images from this book, please visit www.epohl.com.